Emergencies

by Sheila Rivera

first step nonfiction

Lerner Publications · Minneapolis

How do I stay safe in emergencies?

I stay calm.

I tell an adult what happened.

I call 911.

I know my telephone number.

I know my address.

I follow instructions.